DCI

Director of
Central
Intelligence

I0411021

Director of Central Intelligence Directive No. 1/19

Security Policy for Sensitive Compartmented Information and Security Policy Manual

1 March 1995

DIRECTOR OF CENTRAL INTELLIGENCE DIRECTIVE 1/19

SECURITY POLICY FOR
SENSITIVE COMPARTMENTED INFORMATION

(Effective 1 March 1995)

Pursuant to the provisions of National Security Act of 1947 and Executive Order 12333, policies and procedures are hereby established for the security, use, and dissemination of Sensitive Compartmented Information (SCI).

1.0 APPLICABILITY

The controls and procedures in this directive and its supplement, Security Policy Manual for SCI Control Systems, shall be applied by all Intelligence Community agencies. A Senior Official of the Intelligence Community (SOIC) may, for the purpose of SCI protection and DCID implementation, be considered the equivalent of the head of a Cognizant Security Agency (CSA) and may, delegate responsibility for the implementation of policies and procedures defined in an appropriate Director of Central Intelligence Directive (DCID) (e.g., DCID 1/14, 1/19, 1/21) to a Cognizant Security Office. Other programs with special access under the purview of other authorities may at their option, use applicable portions of this DCID for protection of their information and activities. In such cases, the head of the respective department, agency or organization shall be the equivalent of a SOIC for the purposes of this DCID, and may designate a person to act on their behalf for a specific program. Intelligence Community agencies that release or provide SCI to contractors, consultants, or other government departments or agencies shall ensure beforehand that the intended recipients agree to follow these controls and procedures in protection, handling and accountability of SCI.

Policy and procedures in this directive shall be reflected in other Intelligence Community directives related to the security of SCI.

Basic operational protection direction for SCI programs will continue to be prescribed by cognizant executive agents or program directors.

2.0 GENERAL

In order to protect SCI, risk-based analysis should be employed when implementing protection measures. Risk management is essential to balance threat and vulnerabilities with appropriate security measures. This analysis should provide for increased efficiency of operations and co-utilization of facilities wherever practicable.

Specific guidance on what information should be classified and protected as SCI is provided in other documents issued by or pursuant to the authority of the Director of Central Intelligence. Principles and details governing and defining information to be protected by a specific control system shall be included in system manuals and regulations. Such documentation shall also include instructions for decompartmentation, sanitization, release to foreign governments, emergency use (when those actions are feasible and permissible), and additional security policy for the protection of information controlled in SCI subcompartments.

3.0 PROTECTION OF SOURCES AND METHODS

Access to SCI shall be based on need-to-know, formal access approval, and indoctrination. As a general principle, SCI disseminated to persons meeting those criteria shall be provided at the lowest level of classification and compartmentation that will satisfy official requirements applicable to the recipients. Source and method data shall be provided only to the extent necessary to fulfill such requirements. Sanitization of material shall be accomplished to the extent possible to protect against damage to sources and methods through unauthorized disclosure, espionage, or other compromise.

All intelligence production elements shall ensure that the SCI they produce and disseminate excludes, sanitizes, or generalizes, in descending order of preference, source and method data from intelligence products. In support of this, producers of finished intelligence shall:

3.1 Avoid publishing product reports that must be controlled in collection system compartments. When treatment of a particular subject in an intelligence SCI product report requires discussion of operationally compartmented sources and methods, a special supplement, appropriately controlled in compartmented channels, is the preferred approach.

3.2 Ensure that unavoidable references to SCI sources or methods are as nonspecific as practicable. Subject to the provisions of collection system manuals, generalized discussion of compartmented collection capabilities is permitted in finished intelligence products controlled in a product-oriented compartment. Special care shall be taken to ensure that discussion of collection gaps, capabilities to provide indications and warning intelligence, or advice on the reliability of sources in finished intelligence at a relatively low level of compartmentation does not exceed allowable boundaries of SCI control and thereby risk exposure of particularly sensitive SCI to persons lacking need-to-know.

The policy constraint on the use of compartmented information on sources and methods in finished intelligence products applies to all Intelligence Community publications, including the National Intelligence Daily and National Intelligence Estimates. It also applies to all the finished intelligence production of individual agencies, including formal and informal memoranda and studies.

Supplement:
DCI Security Policy Manual
for SCI Control Systems

DCID 1/19 Security Policy Manual

1 March 1995

1.0 INTRODUCTION

This manual contains security policy and procedures common to SCI control system(s) established by the Director of Central Intelligence (DCI) for the protection of classified intelligence information. Users should refer to DCI Directives (DCIDs) and other documents cited herein for guidance on specific security functions. Users are referred to applicable SCI control system manuals or directives for guidance on appropriate classification levels and compartmentation categories.

Questions regarding this manual should be directed to the Director, Community Management Staff (CMS) or successor organization, if not answerable by a Senior Official of the Intelligence Community (SOIC) or his designee of an Intelligence Community (IC) organization.

1.1 Definitions

1.1.1 Accreditation of SCI Facilities (SCIFs)—the formal certification of a specific place referred to as a SCIF that meets prescribed DCID 1/21 physical and technical security standards.

1.1.2 Certified Couriers—individuals whose primary responsibility is to courier SCI material worldwide. The individual must be an active duty military, US Government civilian employee, or contractor meeting DCID 1/14 standards, for that purpose, authorized access to the SCI material they are transporting, or holding a PROXIMITY approval.

1.1.3 Cognizant Security Agency (CSA)—Intelligence organizations or agencies as defined in E.O.12333 have the authority and are responsible for all aspects of security program management with respect to the protection of intelligence sources and methods and for implementation of the DCIDs for activities under their purview. A SOIC is, for the purpose of SCI protection and DCID implementation, considered the equivalent of the head of a CSA or may delegate such responsibility for the implementation of security policies and procedures defined in an appropriate Director of Central Intelligence Directive (DCID) (e.g., DCID 1/14, 1/19, 1/21) to a Cognizant Security Office. Other departments, agencies or organizations may at their option, use applicable portions of this DCID for protection of their information and activities. In such cases, the head of a respective department, agency or organization shall be the equivalent of a SOIC for the purposes of this DCID, and may designate a person to act on their behalf for a specific program.

1.1.4 Cognizant Security Office—The office or offices delegated by the head of a CSA to administer industrial security in a contractor's facility on behalf of the CSA.

1.1.5 Control—the protection procedures mechanism used to regulate or guide the operation. For the purposes of this manual this is defined as, the ability to exercise restraint, direction or influence over; or to provide that degree of physical protection necessary to protect; or measures taken to afford that degree of protect necessary to regulate, handle, manage information or items.

1.1.6 **Data**—any information, regardless of its physical form or characteristics, including, without limitation, written or printed matter; automated information systems (AIS) storage media; maps, charts, paintings, drawings, films, photos, engravings, sketches, working notes, and papers; reproductions of such things by any means or process; and sound, voice, magnetic, or electronic recordings in any form.

1.1.7 **Defensive Travel Security Briefings**—formal advisories that alert traveling personnel of the potential for harassment, exploitation, provocation, capture, entrapment, or criminal activity. These briefings, based upon actual experience when available, include recommended courses of action to mitigate adverse security and personal consequences. The briefings also suggest passive and active measures that personnel should take to avoid becoming targets or inadvertent victims in hazardous areas.

1.1.8 **Designated Couriers**—individuals whose temporary responsibility is to courier SCI material. The individual must be active-duty military, US Government civilian employee, contractor or consultant meeting DCID 1/14 standards, specifically designated for that purpose, authorized access to the SCI material they are transporting, or holding a PROXIMITY approval. They must be familiar with all rules and regulations governing couriers and couriered information, and if applicable, those Federal Aviation Administration and local policies and procedures for screening persons carrying classified material on commercial aircraft.

1.1.9 **Hard Copy Document**—any document that is initially published and distributed by the originating component in physical form and that is not stored or transmitted by electrical means.

1.1.10 **Hazardous Activities**—assignments or visits to and travel through countries designated by the DCI and/or SOIC in accordance with DCID 1/20 or travel in combat zones or other areas in which the threat to US personnel from foreign intelligence services, terrorism, or insurgency is such that the physical safety and security of personnel cannot be reasonably ensured. REF: DCID 1/20 *Security Policy Concerning Travel and Assignment*

1.1.11 **Intelligence Community (and agencies within the Intelligence Community)**—refers to the United States Government agencies and organizations and activities identified in Section 3 of the National Security Act of 1947 and Section 3.4 (f) (1 through 6) of Executive Order 12333.

1.1.12 **Need-to-know**—determination made by an authorized holder of classified information that a prospective recipient requires access to specific classified information in order to perform a lawful and authorized function. Such person shall possess an appropriate security clearance and access approvals in accordance with DCID 1/14.

1.1.13 Raw Intelligence—collected intelligence information that has not yet been converted into finished intelligence.

1.1.14 Risk of Capture Briefings—advisories that alert personnel as to what may be expected in the way of attempts to force or trick them to divulge classified information if captured or detained and that offer suggested courses of action they should follow to avoid or limit such divulgence. These advisories include instructions/advice for advance preparation of innocuous, alternate explanations of duties and background.

1.1.15 SCI Facility (SCIF)—an accredited area, room, group of rooms, buildings, or installation where SCI may be stored, used, discussed, and/or processed.

1.1.16 Senior Intelligence Officer (SIO)—the highest ranking military or civilian individual charged with direct foreign intelligence missions, functions, or responsibilities within a department, agency, component, command, or element of an Intelligence Community organization. When an SIO has been assigned responsibilities under DCID 1/19 or delegated authorities by the SOIC, the SIO is responsible for implementing the policies and procedures of the DCID.

1.1.17 Senior Officials of the Intelligence Community (SOIC)—the head of an agency, office, bureau, or intelligence element listed in Section 3.4(f) (1 through 6) of Executive Order 12333.

1.1.18 Sensitive Compartmented Information (SCI)—classified information concerning or derived from intelligence sources, methods, or analytical processes, which is required to be handled within formal access control systems established by the Director of Central Intelligence.

2.0 PERSONNEL SECURITY

2.1 **General.** The protection of SCI is directly related to the effectiveness of the personnel security program applicable to those individuals having access to such information. An interlocking and mutually supporting series of program elements (e.g., need-to-know, investigation, reinvestigation, and adjudication in accordance with DCID 1/14, *Personnel Security Standards and Procedures Governing Eligibility for Access to Sensitive Compartmented Information,* binding contractual obligations on those granted access, security education and awareness, individual responsibility for observing security requirements and reporting security concerns, and continuing security oversight by supervisory personnel) can provide reasonable assurances against compromise of SCI by those authorized access to it.

2.2 **Need-to-Know Policy.** The primary security principle in safeguarding SCI is to ensure that it is accessible only by those persons with appropriate clearance, access approval, clearly identified need-to-know, and an appropriate indoctrination. Even when approved for a specific access, the holder is expected to practice a need-to-know discipline in acquiring or disseminating information about the program(s) or project(s) involved. Intrinsic to this discipline is acquiring or disseminating only that information essential to effectively carrying out the assignment.

2.3   Standards. Personnel security standards, reporting of data effecting SCI eligibility, investigative requirements, reinvestigations, adjudications, and supervisory security responsibilities shall be in accordance with DCID 1/14.

2.4   SCI Nondisclosure Agreement (NdA). As a condition of access to SCI, individuals must sign a DCI-authorized NdA, which includes a provision for prepublication review. Failure to sign an NdA is cause for denial or revocation of existing SCI access. The NdA establishes explicit obligations on both the government and the individual signer for the protection of SCI.

2.5   Recording Indoctrinations and Debriefings. Briefing officers shall record all SCI indoctrinations and debriefings conducted. Administrative guidance on NdAs, indoctrination and debriefing forms, and related procedures shall be specified by SOICs for areas under their cognizance. This guidance shall ensure that NdAs are retained and retrievable for 70 years after signature.

2.6   Access Approvals. When need-to-know has been established, investigative results have been satisfactorily adjudicated, and an authorized NdA has been signed, SCI access shall be granted and formally recorded. Once a SOIC has determined that an individual is DCID 1/14 eligible without waiver and currently briefed into at least one SCI program, the individual may be approved for additional accesses by any SOIC without further security adjudication. When a previously established need-to-know no longer exists due to reorganization, reassignment, change in duties or any other reason, the SCI access approval(s) affected by this change in need-to-know shall be canceled, and the individual involved shall be debriefed.

2.6.1   Authority. SCI access approvals shall be granted by the SOIC having cognizance of the persons involved. In addition, for persons in non-National Foreign Intelligence Board (NFIB) government organizations, SCI access approvals are granted by the DCI through the CIA. Unless specifically delegated, approval authority for access to certain operational collection systems is retained by the cognizant program manager, executive agent, or national authority. SOICs are responsible for issuing administrative procedures governing the granting of SCI accesses in their organizations.

2.6.2   General SCI Approvals. "PROXIMITY" approvals may be granted by the cognizant SOIC to persons who closely support SCI collection, processing, or use SCI but whose duties do not warrant granting operational or product-oriented SCI access approvals, with the requisite substantive indoctrination. PROXIMITY allows the holders to perform their duties in support of any SCI control system provided the tasks do not involve visual or aural access to clear text, intelligible SCI.

2.6.2.1 PROXIMITY approvals may also be granted, according to the criteria in 2.6.2.2 below, when a person is authorized one or more SCI control systems. For example, substantive access to COMINT may be required even though PROXIMITY is appropriate for other SCI access.

2.6.2.2 Minimum criteria for PROXIMITY approvals are:

2.6.2.2.1 The nature of the person's support to SCI involves a substantial latent risk of exposure to SCI through inadvertence or a deliberate effort by the individual.

2.6.2.2.2 Approval for a specific SCI system or project would provide the person more information than needed, either through the indoctrination or by virtue of the access approval, or both.

2.6.2.2.3 The person does not need to know substantive SCI in order to perform his or her function and will not receive access in the normal course of his or her duties.

2.6.2.2.4 The person's potential for access is such that personnel security assurances provided through investigations and adjudication for collateral clearances are not deemed adequate by the cognizant SOIC or designee.

2.6.2.3 Persons determined by their SOIC to require PROXIMITY approvals shall be processed to DCID 1/14 personnel security standards. They shall be given a non-SCI-revealing briefing notifying them that their duties may bring them in proximity to highly sensitive government information; cautioning them to report to their security officer any inadvertent access involving them; and, where appropriate, providing them a generalized description of the appearance of SCI documents (e.g., material may have color-coded cover sheets and will bear handling system caveats) to enable them to recognize such material if it is exposed to them. (The NdA mentions "special access" not SCI.)

2.6.2.4 NdAs are required of persons being granted PROXIMITY approvals to obligate them to observe the agreement's provisions with respect to any classified to which they might gain knowledge. If an inadvertent disclosure is made to an individual with PROXIMITY approval, that person shall be given a defensive security briefing to ensure he or she understands the applicability of the NdA and the obligations under it.

2.6.2.5 Once granted, PROXIMITY approvals are valid within the cognizance of the granting SOIC.

2.6.2.6 To the extent that SOICs find it practicable, persons already holding substantive access approvals may be converted to PROXIMITY if they qualify. Those converted shall be cautioned not to discuss with other PROXIMITY-approved persons their previously acquired knowledge of SCI. SOICs are expected to exercise prudence in extending PROXIMITY approvals to persons and positions not now requiring SCI access approvals in order to avoid undue burden on the SCI personnel security system. Processing of substantive access approval request will normally take precedence over PROXIMITY requests.

2.7 **Central SCI Database.** A community wide SCI database will be maintained by the DCI. The DCI will ensure the database is maintained in a format that will permit the integration with or expansion into a U.S. government wide clearance data base.

2.8 **Security Indoctrination and Education**

2.8.1 Prior to signing the NdA or being afforded access to SCI, persons approved for SCI access shall be given a non-SCI-revealing briefing on the general nature and procedures for protecting the SCI to which they will be exposed, advised of their obligations both to protect that information and to report matters of security concern, and allowed to express any reservations concerning the NdA or access to SCI. Persons who are unwilling to sign the NdA or to accept SCI security obligations shall not be granted SCI access.

2.8.2 Prepublication review is required for classification and policy review prior to public release of SCI related information. Such prepublication review is also necessary to avoid potential damage that would result from confirmation of previously published information containing SCI. The indoctrination shall instruct persons that such damage may be aggravated when written and they may not publicly cite such information especially in conjunction with military title, U.S. Government position, or contractual relationship with SCI programs. All persons granted SCI access shall be advised periodically of their continuing security responsibilities and of security threats they may encounter. Annex C to DCID 1/14, *Standards for Security Awareness Programs in the US Intelligence Community, provides guidance.*

2.8.3 Subsequent to signing the NdA, persons shall be fully indoctrinated on the aspects of the SCI to which they are authorized access and for which they have a demonstrated need-to-know. The indoctrination will describe the systems to which access is granted, cite the specific aspects of the system requiring protection, and advise the recipient of proper channels for reporting matters of security significance, requesting security advice, and determining whether others are authorized access to the system(s) for which the recipient is approved. The indoctrination will be structured to inform the recipient of the sensitivity of the information and appropriate cautions concerning answers to questions from nonbriefed persons, such as family, personal associates, media and journalists.

2.9 **Foreign Contacts.** Close, continuing personal associations with foreign nationals by persons approved for SCI access are of security concern. Persons with SCI access shall be informed of their continuing responsibility to report to their SCI security officers all close and continuing contact with foreign nationals, or any contact with representatives or citizens of foreign countries that is considered threatening or suspicious. SCI-indoctrinated persons are also responsible for reporting contacts with persons from other countries whenever those persons show undue or persistent interest in employment, assignment, or sensitive national security matters. Contacts, or failure to report contacts, in either of the above situations shall result in reevaluation of eligibility for continued SCI access by the cognizant SOIC. Casual contacts, which do not fall within either of the above situations, normally need not be reported.

2.10 SCI Travel and Assignment Security Policy. Persons currently approved for SCI access who plan unofficial travel to or through, or who are being assigned to duty in, foreign countries and areas incur a special security obligation. This includes requirements to provide advance notice of unofficial travel and receive appropriate defensive security briefings prior to official assignment or unofficial travel. Security policy applicable to such travel or assignment is stated in DCID 1/20, *Security Policy Concerning Travel and Assignment of Personnel with Access to SCI.*

3.0 PHYSICAL SECURITY

3.1 Construction and Protection Standards. All SCI must be stored within accredited SCIFs. Accrediting authorities are responsible for ensuring that SCIFs are established only when there are clear operational requirements for them and when existing SCIFs are not adequate to support the requirement. The requirements justifying a new SCIF shall be documented and maintained with accreditation records. Physical security standards for the construction and protection of such facilities are prescribed in the current DCID 1/21, *Physical Security Standards for Sensitive Compartmented Information.*

3.2 Accreditation of SCIFs. The DCI has responsibility for all SCIF accreditation and can delegate that authority. Except where specific agreement exists, introduction of an additional program into a previously accredited SCIF requires the joint approval of the host SOIC and the responsible SOIC requesting tenant status.

The CIA shall accredit SCIFs for executive branch departments and agencies outside the Intelligence Community, and for the legislative and judicial branches.

The DCI, or the SOIC conducting an SCI program with a foreign government, will accredit the SCIF for that foreign government, or as specified in the program security manual.

3.2.1 Co-utilization of SCIFs is encouraged to promote efficiency, achieve economies, and reduce proliferation of SCIFs. However, the efficiency of co-utilizations should never abrogate the need-to-know principle. In co-use situations, non-related and/or non-SCI activities within a SCIF must:

3.2.1.1 Have the approval of the accrediting SOIC in advance;

3.2.1.2 Be governed by a Memorandum of Understanding (MOU) which may be a hard copy or an electronic communication fully identifying all approving authorities;

3.2.1.3 Be physically separated from each other at all times to avoid disclosure of information relating to respective programs;

3.2.1.4 Assure that all persons working on non-SCI activities are approved to DCID 1/14 standards and be given a non-SCI revealing briefing (see section 2.6.2.3) after meeting the minimum criteria for PROXIMITY Approval;

3.2.1.5 The accrediting authority for the SCIF at the time of the MOU remains the overall authority for the SCIF unless all parties concerned agree to transfer such responsibility to another agency. If a transfer of accreditation or responsibility occurs, IC organizations must be officially notified and the accreditation data and facility security profile transferred to the new CSA. Reaccreditation of the SCIF is not required provided the transferred documentation includes certification that the SCIF meets DCID 1/21 standards and identifies any waivers. Acceptance of the accreditation certification does not relieve the new CSA of responsibility for ensuring compliance with applicable SCI security requirements, however, changes to the current SCIF may not exceed the standards established in DCID 1/21 without the concurrence of the SOIC and approval of the DCI.

3.2.1.6 The MOU for a SCIF must, as a minimum, identify the CSA responsible for the general security of the SCIF, the compartmentation and classification level of SCI authorized for storage, special security procedures for the SCIF, security and support services each user requires, and how user requirements will be satisfied. The accrediting authority retains ultimate responsibility for the security, physical inspections, and internal operation of the SCIF.

3.2.2 The CSA responsible for accreditation of the SCIF must approve all physical modifications of the SCIF and be notified before automated information systems or other forms of electronic equipment and processing system within the SCIF are added or changed. Before using such equipment for SCI, those introducing the equipment must ensure appropriate authorities must accredit or authorize use of the equipment, as required by the DCID 1/16 supplement, *Security Manual for Uniform Protection of Intelligence Processed in Automated Information Systems and Networks*, dated 19 July 1988, or successor policy statements.

3.3 **Emergency Plans.** An emergency plan shall be developed, approved and maintained for each accredited SCIF. This may be part of an overall department, agency, or installation plan, so long as it satisfactorily addresses the considerations stated below. Emergency planning shall take account of fire, natural disaster, labor strife, entrance of emergency personnel (e.g., host country police and firemen) into a SCIF, and the physical protection of those working in such SCIFs. Planning should address the adequacy of protection and fire-fighting equipment, of evacuation plans for persons and SCI, and of life-support equipment (e.g. oxygen and masks) that might be required.

3.3.1 In areas where political instability, terrorism, host country attitudes, or criminal activity suggests the possibility that a SCIF might be overrun by hostile forces, emergency plans must provide for the secure destruction/removal of SCI under adverse circumstances, to include such eventualities as loss of electrical power, non-availability of open spaces for burning or chemical decomposition of material, and immediate action to be taken if faced with mob attack. Where the risk of overrun is significant, SCI holdings must be reduced to, and kept at, an absolute minimum needed for current working purposes, with reference or background material to be obtained, when needed, from other activities and returned or destroyed when it has served its purpose.

3.3.2 Emergency plans shall be reviewed annually and updated as necessary. All personnel shall be familiar with the plans. In areas where political or criminal activity suggests the possibility that the SCIF might be overrun, drills shall be conducted as circumstances warrant, but no less frequently than annually, to ensure testing and adequacy of plans.

4.0 TECHNICAL SECURITY

4.1 **Technical Surveillance Countermeasures.** Responsible SOICs shall ensure that technical surveillance countermeasures are conducted at their SCIFs, domestic or foreign, in accordance with DCID 1/22, *Technical Surveillance Countermeasures, (TSCM)* and DCI procedural guides issued in accordance with DCID 1/22. (Overseas facilities require initial TSCM.) Briefings on technical penetration threats shall be provided to personnel working within SCIFs.

4.2 **Compromising Emanations Control Security (TEMPEST).** All equipment used to transmit, handle, or process SCI electronically, including communications, word processing, VCRs, TV monitors, facsimile machine, and automated information systems equipment, must satisfy the requirements of NTISSP 300, *National Telecommunications and Information Systems Security Policy and NTISSI 7000, TEMPEST Countermeasures for Facilities* (or successor policies) in the most efficient, cost effective manner possible.

4.3 **Automated Information Systems (AIS) Security.** All AIS and networks used for processing, handling, or storing SCI shall be operated and secured in compliance with DCID 1/16, *Security Policy for Uniform Protection of Intelligence Processed in Automated Information Systems and Networks* or successor document.

5.0 SCI INFORMATION SERVICES CENTERS AND SECURITY OFFICIALS

5.1 **SCI Special Security Offices and/or Control Centers.** SCI Special Security Offices and/or Control Centers, as appropriate, shall be established to serve as the focal point(s) for the receipt, control, and accountability of SCI, and other SCI security functions for one or more SCIFs in the local area. The number of such offices and/or centers shall be determined locally on the basis of practicality, number of SCIFs to be serviced and organizations involved.

5.2 **SCI Special Security/Control Officers.** Appropriately SCI-indoctrinated special security officers and/or SCI control officers and alternates thereto, shall be designated to operate each SCI Special Security Office and/or Control Center. Such officials shall normally have day-to-day SCI security cognizance over their offices/centers and subordinate SCIFs, if any, for that SCI authorized to be handled by organizations served by them. Responsible SOICs shall ensure appropriate training in SCI security policy and procedures is provided their SCI special security/control officers and other SCI registry/security personnel. SCI Special Security/Control Officers shall provide advice and assistance on SCI matters to their organizations and other activities being supported, consistent with specific responsibilities assigned by their SOICs. This may include one or more of the following:

5.2.1 Ensuring that SCI is properly controlled, transmitted, destroyed, packaged, safeguarded and where appropriate, brought under accountability.

5.2.2 Giving advice and guidance on SCI classification matters, sanitization, downgrading, decompartmentation, and operational use.

5.2.3 Ensuring that SCI is disseminated only to persons authorized access to the material involved and having an established need-to-know.

5.2.4 Conducting or managing required SCI personnel and physical security actions and procedures.

5.2.5 Investigating SCI security infractions and preparing reports and recommendations as required.

5.2.6 Conducting required interface with SCI telecommunications centers, AIS facilities, and similar offices to ensure SCI security. Interaction between SCI Special Security/Control Officers and Information Systems Security Officers (ISSOs), appointed pursuant to DCID 1/16, is particularly important in ensuring the security of both SCIFs and the AIS network components housed in SCIFs.

6.0 INFORMATION SECURITY

6.1 **Standard Classification Marking Requirements.** Standard security classification markings (to include classification authority and declassification markings) shall be applied to SCI according to the Executive Order 12356 *National Security Information* or successor document and Executive Branch implementing directives. Classification guides issued by program managers shall be used in classifying SCI. **NOTE: Section 6.4.3 specifies waiver situations when the sponsoring SOIC deems them appropriate based upon the nature of the material and the protection it is being afforded.**

6.2 **SCI Caveats, Codewords, and Designators.** The bottoms of all pages of SCI hard copy documents shall be marked with the applicable SCI control system caveats. The front and back covers of bound documents shall also be appropriately marked with the proper SCI system caveats. Whenever practicable, front and back covers shall bear the color code bar(s) for the system(s). If the material is to be controlled in only one SCI control system, mark it as follows:

"HANDLE VIA (name of SCI control system) CHANNELS ONLY"

If the material is to be controlled in two or more SCI control systems, mark it as follows:

"HANDLE VIA (names of SCI control systems) CHANNELS JOINTLY"

Mark SCI codewords or operational program designators along with the security classification on all pages requiring SCI protection. Codewords and program designators are to be placed after the classification at tops and bottoms of pages.

6.2.1 Digraphs and Trigraphs. It is DCI policy that digraphs and trigraphs are normally unclassified. There are circumstances that may require classification. Before a di/trigraph is classified, a threat assessment identifying the risk of unclassified use must be made. The SOIC must approve classification in the appropriate classification guide. SCI briefed personnel are required to be cognizant of operational security concerns and potential classification when di/trigraphs are associated with program information, activities, or locations. Di/trigraphs should be disclosed only to personnel who understand the sensitivity and requirement for appropriate protection.

6.3 Dissemination Control Markings. When applicable to their information content, SCI documents shall be marked with the dissemination control markings in the manner prescribed by DCID 1/7, *Security Controls on the Dissemination of Intelligence Information.*

6.4 Portion Marking. Each copy of an SCI document shall, by marking or other means, indicate: (1) which portions are classified, with the applicable classification level, and which portions are not classified; and (2) which portions require SCI codewords, caveats, program designators, or DCID 1/7 control markings.

6.4.1 Security protection requirements of portions shall be shown by abbreviations for classifications (i.e.,"TS," "S," and "C," in descending order; "U" to designate unclassified items); authorized abbreviations for SCI control system caveats; authorized digraph, trigraph, or other recognized abbreviations for codewords; product or project indicators; and DCID 1/7 control marking short abbreviations. Portion markings shall be placed immediately following the portion letter or number, or in the absence of sections, parts, paragraphs or sub-paragraphs, at the beginning of unnumbered paragraphs, and after main titles that stand alone.

6.4.2 Alternatively, such as in the case of documents all portions of which are of the same level of classification and control, a paragraph or statement on the document may be used to indicate the security protection requirements of document portions. Unless the usefulness of the document would suffer thereby, titles of SCI documents shall be so worded as to avoid the need for compartmented control and to minimize or eliminate the need for classification.

6.4.3 With DCI approval and in compliance with the Executive Order 12356 *National Security Information* or successor document, SOICs may grant waivers of the portion marking requirements for government and contractor-generated SCI when deemed necessary to alleviate an extreme administrative and/or cost burden. Waivers shall not be considered for any permanently valuable records of the government. Any information transmitted outside the facility, where it may be used as a source document in the derivative classification of other information, must be portion marked before its transmittal. Further, any document upon which the waiver is exercised shall be marked as follows:

6.5 **Letters or Memoranda of Transmittal and Facsimile Transmission.**

6.5.1 **SCI Transmittal Letters/Memoranda.** Mark transmittal letters/memoranda that contain SCI but which transmit SCI of another category with the highest classification of the letter/memorandum and its enclosure(s)/attachment(s). any SCI caveats and/or codewords that apply to the transmittal letter/memorandum itself, and a notation such as:

"CONTAINS (*) INFORMATION"
(* = classification, caveat(s)/codeword(s)
as applicable to the enclosed/attached material only)

"REGRADE AS (**)
(** = classification, caveat(s)/codeword(s)
applicable to the transmittal letter/memorandum only)
WHEN SEPARATED FROM ENCLOSURE(S)/ATTACHMENT(S)"

When applicable, the transmittal letter/memorandum itself must bear a Document Accountability Number (DAN) consistent with the SCI it contains (see section 6.6). The package of the transmittal letter/memorandum and its enclosure(s)/attachment(s) must bear an SCI cover sheet (see section 6.8) that reflects the classification and all SCI caveats/codewords applicable to the package. The cover sheet shall bear a DAN assigned in accordance with the established precedence of SCI systems.

6.5.2 **Classified or Unclassified Transmittal Letters/Memoranda.** Mark transmittal letters/memoranda that contain classified information, but no SCI, or which are unclassified, with the highest classification of the letter/memorandum and its enclosure(s) attachments(s) and a notation such as:

"CONTAINS (classification,caveat(s)/codeword(s)) INFORMATION"

"REGRADE AS (classification)
**WHEN SEPARATED FROM ENCLOSURE(S)/ATTACHMENT(S)" or
"UNCLASSIFIED WHEN ENCLOSED/ATTACHED SCI DOCUMENTS
ARE REMOVED"** (as applicable to the contents of the letter/memorandum itself)

The transmittal letter/memorandum should identify the originating registry, as appropriate. An SCI cover sheet appropriate to the enclosure(s)/attachment(s) should be placed on the package of the transmittal letter/memorandum and its enclosure(s)/attachment(s). The cover sheet shall bear accountability numbers as appropriate.

6.5.3 **Header Sheets.** Conspicuously mark the top and bottom of individual header sheets used to precede the transmission of SCI material by secure facsimile with the highest security classification of the transmitted material. Appropriate SCI caveats, and/or DCID 1/7 control markings shall be prominently marked on header sheets. Where applicable, SCI documents transmitted by secure facsimile shall be marked and accounted for in the same manner as hard copy documents.

6.6 **SCI Document Accountability Numbers (DAN).** Originators shall assign a DAN to those SCI documents **approved by the SOIC as accountable.** Blocks of numbers will be assigned to SOIC's by the CIA or by a SOIC's SCI Information Services Center (as appropriate). DANs shall be placed in the designated block on cover sheets, on the front cover and title page (if any), and all succeeding pages. Any retrieval or configuration management number used for information management purposes may be assigned to a document but should not be considered a security control or protection mechanism.

6.6.1 Each DAN shall consist of an identifiable character of the applicable control system, a six-digit number selected on a "one up" basis from the block of numbers assigned to the control office, and the last two digits of the current year, separated by a hyphen. When a document contains SCI subject to two or more control systems, assign a DAN according to the established precedence of SCI systems. For example, material containing TK and COMINT would be assigned a TCS number.

6.6.2 If a DAN is used, a copy number must be assigned to individual documents. In addition, copy numbers along with the DAN must be properly displayed on the cover or on page 1 of the document. The copy number can be a combination of digits and/or letters to show reproduced copies, such as Series B, Copy 1, Copy 2, ect.

6.7 **Specialized Media Labeling Requirements for SCI.**

6.7.1 **Automated Information Systems (AIS) Media.** Each item [e.g. demountable data and program storage medium (magnetic tape, disk pack, floppy disk, magnetic cassette, compact disk, etc.), card deck, punched paper tape] shall be externally labeled with the highest classification and most restrictive category of information ever recorded thereon until the media are sanitized or declassified (see para 6.1.4). Internal AIS media identification shall include security markings in a form suitable for the media (i.e., classification; SCI system caveats, codewords, product indicators; and DCID 1/7 control markings, if applicable).

6.7.2 **Photographic Media and Video Tape.** Photography in roll, flat, or other form and video tape containing SCI shall be labeled with its classification and applicable SCI control system caveats or codewords. For film in roll form, a label itemizing the required data shall be placed on the end of the spool flange, on the side of the spool container, and on the container cover (if any). If the flange label is visible through the container, no outside labeling is required. Roll film and video tape shall include head and tail sequences and all security markings applicable to the contents. Positive film flats or slides shall bear individual internal markings showing the classification and all applicable SCI and other control markings. The frames of slides shall also be labeled with the classification and applicable SCI caveats and codewords (which may be abbreviated if necessary to fit in the space provided).

6.7.3 Microform Media.

6.7.3.1 Microfiche. Each microfiche shall have a heading, the elements of which are readable without magnification, that provides the document title (which may be abbreviated), abbreviated classification, SCI DAN if applicable, and, using standard abbreviations, applicable SCI caveats and codewords and DCID 1/7 control markings by color or other immediately recognizable means, where practicable. Individual microfiche shall be placed in color-coded envelopes indicative of the SCI control system(s) applicable to the informational contents.

6.7.3.2 Microfilm. Each roll of microfilm shall contain classification and control information at the beginning and end of the roll. This may be in abbreviated form. Boxes containing processed film on reels and film cartridges shall be labeled to show the document title (generic title if more than one document is on the film), the highest security classification of the contents, the SCI caveats and codewords applicable to the filmed information, and any DCID 1/7 control markings that may apply.

6.7.4 Electronically Transmitted Information. SCI transmitted by accredited electrical or electronic means resulting in record copy material shall be marked at the top and bottom of each page (to include each segment of messages printed on perforated paper) with its security classification, and labeled to show all applicable SCI caveats, codewords and product designators, and any DCID 1/7 control markings that apply. These markings shall be clearly shown consistent with the design of the message format being used except that the overall classification and applicable SCI caveat or codewords(s) and product indicator(s), and DCID 1/7 control markings shall precede the text of the message. Section 6.1 on classification/declassification marking and section 6.4 on portion marking shall be applied in the case of record SCI traffic. SCI documents transmitted by secure facsimile are not messages. They shall be marked and accounted for the same as if they were hard copy documents (see section 6.5.3 for guidance).

6.7.5 Hard Copy Files, Folders, or Groups of Documents. Hard Copy files, folders, or groups of documents shall be conspicuously marked to ensure the protection of all SCI contained therein. Such material shall be marked on the file folder tab or other prominent location, or have an appropriate SCI cover sheet affixed.

6.7.6 Graphic Arts Materials. Visual aids, maps, art work, blueprints, videos, etc. shall be marked with the assigned classification and applicable SCI control system or codewords under the legend, title block, or scale, and at the top and bottom in such a manner as to be reproduced on all copies.

6.8 Cover Sheets. When it is necessary to guard against unauthorized disclosure to persons not possessing appropriate SCI accesses, separate cover sheets shall be used on SCI documents. When sending SCI material to another agency, appropriate cover sheets shall be used. Cover sheets shall show, by color or other immediately recognizable format or legend, what SCI control system or combination of systems apply, the classification, and other applicable markings.

6.9 SCI Policy. It is the DCI's policy to eliminate document accountability as a routine security protection measure. SCI security or control officers responsible for SCIFs shall maintain records, manual or electronic (bar codes), of external receipt and dispatch sufficient to investigate loss or compromises of SCI documents during transmittal.

    6.9.1 Accountable SCI — that SCI information determined by the SOIC or designee to be of critical enough sensitivity to require the most stringent protection methods, including traceability and audit.

        6.9.1.1 Approval Authority. SOICs are authorized to approve document accountability, in writing, on specific highly sensitive program information within SCI. This authority may not be delegated. An annual report of accountable authorizations, volume, and cost may be required at the request of the DCI.

        6.9.1.2 Records for Incoming Accountable SCI. Except as provided in section 6.9.3, a record shall be kept of accountable SCI documents received by a SCIF. Records shall identify the material by DAN and copy number, originator, a brief description of the material, and the identity of an individual or office(s) within the SCIF that received the material. This will normally be satisfied by maintaining records including electronic bar codes that provide necessary identifying data. Accountability of electronically generated hardcopy accountable data (e.g. faxes, E-mail, or records message traffic) may be fulfilled through any record system maintained for other hard copy documents.

        Material which has been designated as accountable by the SOIC, shall be controlled in order to comply with the requirements of Section 6.11.

        6.9.1.3 Outgoing Accountable SCI. Except as provided in section 6.9.3, a manual or electronic receipt or equivalent record, shall be retained for two years for all accountable SCI physically dispatched from the SCIF. Receipts shall identify the material by DAN, copy number, and originator; contain a brief description of the material; and identify the recipient (individual or office). For Confidential COMINT-related material, this requirement may be fulfilled through the required Defense Courier System (DCS) pouch or package receipt or by other appropriate dissemination records kept by the sender.

6.9.2 Non-accountable SCI. Accountability records (e.g. internal receipting among activities in the same SCIF, access records, destruction certificates) are not required for non-accountable SCI data. External receipts and dispatch records shall be maintained to ensure documents are not lost in transmission.

6.9.3 Working Material. Accountability records are not required for SCI working materials used exclusively within a SCIF. Such materials must be safeguarded according to the handling, storage, and disposition requirements for accountable SCI documents; marked "Working Papers—Destroy within 90 days", and must be destroyed within 90 days of origin or placed in formal SCI control channels. SOICs may grant waivers of the 90-day period.

6.10 Temporary Release of SCI Outside a SCIF. When operational needs require SCI to be released for processing or temporary use by SCI-indoctrinated persons in non-SCI-accredited areas, such release shall only be accomplished with the consent and under the supervision of the responsible SCI security/control officer. The responsible officer shall obtain signed receipts for SCI released in this manner and shall ensure that conditions of use will provide adequate security until the SCI is returned to SCIF.

6.11 Audits and Inventories for Accountable Documents. SOICs shall arrange for SCI security/control officers, to conduct such periodic reviews of SCI held by organizations under their cognizance, and will ensure that proper accountability is being maintained and that SCI is destroyed when no longer needed. SOICs may require the inventory of accountable SCI within activities under their cognizance.

6.12 Reproduction. Reproduction of SCI documents shall be kept to a minimum consistent with operational necessity. Copies of documents are subject to the same control, accountability, and destruction procedures as the originals. Stated prohibitions against reproduction shall be honored. CSAs will ensure that equipment used for SCI reproduction is thoroughly inspected and sanitized before equipment is removed from a SCIF.

6.13 Transportation/Transmission. SCI shall be transmitted from one SCIF to another in a manner that ensures it is properly protected. Material hand-carried by a courier shall be transported in an approved container discretely marked with a notation such as **"PROPERTY OF THE US GOVERNMENT—TO BE RETURNED UNOPENED TO** (name of appropriate organization and telephone number that will be manned at all times)." A briefcase with a locking device can serve as an outer wrapper. No inner wrapper is required if SCI is transported between SCIFs within the same building. If a briefcase is used, an unobtrusive luggage tag will be used and contain the aforementioned notation/information.

6.13.1 Courier Procedures. SCI may be carried from one SCIF to another by certified or designated courier(s) approved for this purpose, by diplomatic pouch, or by the DCS. One person may serve as a courier; however, the responsible senior security officer or designee should assess circumstances such as volume of material, mode of travel, high crime area, sensitivity, etc. which would indicate that more than one person would be prudent to ensure continuous custody and protection of the material. Designated couriers should only be used for time critical/time sensitive data in those cases where certified couriers cannot satisfy requirements. Courier procedures shall ensure that SCI materials shall be handled only by individuals determined to be DCID 1/14 eligible, and will ensure that the materials are protected against the possibility of hijacking, loss, exposure to unauthorized persons, or other forms of compromise.

6.13.2 Wrapping Procedures. SCI shall be enclosed for shipment in two opaque envelopes or be otherwise suitably double-wrapped using approved containers. Outer containers shall be secured by an approved means that reasonably protect against surreptitious access. The inner and outer containers shall be annotated to show the package number and addresses of the sending and receiving SCIF. The notation **"TO BE OPENED BY THE** (appropriate SCI Special Security Control Officer)" shall be placed above the pouch address of the receiving SCIF on the inner container. The inner wrapper shall contain the document receipt and the name of the person or activity for whom the material is intended. The applicable security classification and the legend **"CONTAINS SENSITIVE COMPARTMENTED INFORMATION"** shall appear on each side of the inner wrapper only.

6.13.3 Electronic Transmissions. Senders of SCI transmitted electrically or electronically (to include facsimile, computer, secure voice, E-mail, or any other means of telecommunication), must ensure that such transmissions are made only to authorized recipients. Recipients must provide proper protection for SCI so received. Electronic transmission of SCI shall be limited to specifically designated and accredited communications circuits secured by an NSA-approved cryptographic system and/or protected distribution systems. The construction and protection of SCI telecommunications facilities shall be as prescribed in DCID 1/21 and NACSI 4000-series publications or successor publication documents.

6.14 Destruction of SCI. SCI shall be retained for the time periods specified in records control schedules approved by the Archivist of the United States (44 U.S.C. 33 and FPMR 101-11.4). Destruction Records for an **accountable** SCI document shall be retained in a master record. Duplicate information and other non-recorded copies of SCI documents shall be destroyed as soon as possible after their purpose has been served. Destruction shall be accomplished in a manner that will preclude reconstruction in intelligible form. Only those DCI approved methods (e.g., burning, pulping, shredding, pulverizing, melting, or chemical decomposition, depending on the type of material to be destroyed) specifically authorized may be used. Destruction of data shall be assured by an appropriately indoctrinated person(s). For situations such as high volume or bulk destruction of accountable data, or when the destruction of accountable data is external to a SCIF, the responsible senior security officer or designee may determine that two personnel are appropriate. SCI in computer or automated information systems or other magnetic media shall be "destroyed" through erasure by approved degaussing equipment or by executing sanitization procedures specified in the *Guide to Understanding Data Remanence in Automated Information Systems*, (NCSC-TG-025), September 1991, or successor publication.

7.0 CONTRACTOR/CONSULTANT SECURITY

7.1 **Policy.** Basic DCI policy on release of foreign intelligence to contractors and consultants (hereinafter contractors) is contained in paragraph 7, of DCID 1/7, *Security Controls on Dissemmination of Intelligence Information.* Specific release provisions should be included in any control system manuals and regulations. SCI may be released by SOICs to U.S. Government contractors according to the following instructions.

7.1.1 The release, control, handling, accountability, and destruction of SCI shall be accomplished pursuant to the provisions of DCID 1/7 and this manual. The permission of the originator of the information to be released shall be obtained in compliance with DCID 1/7. (If necessary, this permission may be granted in the form of lateral agreements between departments and agencies.)

7.1.2 The sponsoring agency or department shall prescribe as part of the contractual arrangement the security requirements for safeguarding SCI according to this directive DCID 1/19. This may include a requirement that the contractor or consultant establish and maintain SCIF(s). All activities involving SCI (including discussions) shall be conducted in a SCIF. Exceptions may be approved for manufacturing and operational activities based on security provisions tailored to the specific threat to the activity.

7.1.3 The security portions of contracts for work involving SCI shall include detailed guidance to the contractor concerning the use of references to SCI accesses, even by unclassified acronyms in advertising or recruitment media. In general, references to SSBI (Single Scope Background Investigation) will be allowed in these venues while references to SCI per se will be allowed or denied, on a case by case basis. Guidance will be based on the contractor's total situation (size, heterogeneity of technical population, product lines, etc.) along with the realization that such media provides foreign intelligence services a ready basis for targeting activities. Failure to comply with any prohibition against recruitment should be considered a breach of contract, and will also be considered a security violation.

7.1.4 SOICs of the sponsoring agency or department shall perform, or have performed, security surveys at contractor or consultant SCIFs and accredit the SCIF, prior to release of SCI. The purpose of the survey is to determine that the SCIF and security procedures established by the contractor or consultant are adequate for the protection of SCI. If it meets SCI standards, the SCIF shall be accredited for the SCI program(s) involved. When a SOIC assumes cognizance of an already accredited SCIF, the SOIC may accept an earlier security survey as the basis for his accreditation provided there have been no significant changes to the SCIF in the intervening period and the survey is not more than three years old. Thereafter, physical security inspections to ensure continuous compliance with SCI security requirements shall be conducted, in accordance with DCID 1/21.

7.1.5 Decisions on selection of contractors for SCI activities must take into account the contractor's past record in properly safeguarding classified material.

7.1.6 SCIFs established in industry must be monitored by the sponsoring SOIC to ensure that SCI security procedures are followed and that SCI documents are properly segregated from other materials held by the contractor. When two or more organizations release SCI to a given contractor which will be used within the same SCIF, the organizations shall execute a MOU defining each organizations' SCI security responsibilities.

7.1.7 With respect to SCI contractor visit requests, it is the responsibility of the US Government contracting officer or the department or agency sponsoring the visit to:

    7.1.7.1 Establish a valid need-to-know for the contractor's visit; and

    7.1.7.2 Permit certification of the contractor's SCI access(es) by either the government program security officer or the contractor security officer holding the accesses.

7.2 Foreign Ownership, Control, or Influence (FOCI).

(This Section remains the same as found in DCID 1/19 dated 19 February 1987. Any changes in FOCI are to be determined by the Security Policy Board and will be incorporated at a later date.)

8.0 LEGISLATIVE BRANCH ACCESS TO SCI

8.1 Policy

8.1.2 As a basic principle, access to intelligence information shall be consistent with the protection of intelligence sources and methods. Normally, Congressional requests for intelligence information can be satisfied at the collateral (i.e., non-SCI) level, but, in certain instances, there may be a need for access to SCI. In these instances, every effort shall be made to exclude, to the extent possible, data on intelligence sources and methods.

8.1.3 Members of Congress may be provided access to SCI on a need-to-know basis without a security investigation or adjudication after appropriate indoctrination. Heads of organizations within the Intelligence Community or Program Managers providing SCI shall provide indoctrination briefings on the sensitivity and vulnerability of the information, and the sources and methods involved, as required to ensure proper protection. Documentation relative to the passing of clearances should include the fact of, or convey the status of, appropriate clearance/access indoctrination.

8.1.4 Access to SCI by staff members of the Senate Select Committee on Intelligence (SSCI) and the House Permanent Select Committee on Intelligence (HPSCI) are governed by Memoranda of Understanding executed by the Chairmen of these Committees and the DCI. Provision of information and materials to these Committees shall be in accordance with mutually agreed arrangements.

8.1.5 Requests for SCI access approvals for other legislative branch personnel shall be referred to the Director of the Office of Congressional Affairs (OCA) for DCI approval. Requests must be in writing by committee or sub-committee chairmen and clearly describe the nominee's need-to-know. Issues arising with regard to particular requests shall be referred to the DCI for resolution. Unless otherwise authorized by the DCI, approval for SCI access for legislative branch staff personnel shall be limited to:

8.1.5.1 Permanent staff personnel of appropriate Congressional committees and subcommittees;

8.1.5.2 Selected employees of the General Accounting Office and the Library of Congress; and

8.1.5.3 Selected members of the staffs of the leadership of the House and Senate, as agreed by the DCI and the leadership.

8.2 Verification Requirement. The DCI's OCA will verify, in coordination with program managers and on behalf of the DCI, the need of persons in the legislative branch, other than members of Congress, for SCI access. Verifications shall be based on such persons' job responsibilities in the following areas:

8.2.1 Direct involvement in authorization legislation pertaining to IC organizations;

8.2.2 Direct involvement in appropriations legislation for IC organizations;

8.2.3 Direct involvement in reviews authorized by law of activities of IC organizations; and

8.2.4 Direct involvement in other legislative matters which, of necessity, require direct SCI access.

8.3 Access Approval Procedures

8.3.1 SCI access approvals may be granted to staff personnel in the legislative branch, described above, who possess a Top Secret collateral clearance and who meet the investigative standards set forth in DCID 1/14. Requests for exceptions to this policy shall be referred to the DCI's Director of OCA. The requester of the SCI access approval is responsible for having a DCID 1/14-scope investigation conducted. Security organizations involved in processing requests for investigations on legislative branch staff personnel should be alert to guard against error that could arise from investigative records being held by different agencies or from uncertainty about the clearances/access approvals held by staff personnel. Adequate records of investigations and clearances should be kept and updated. Reports of investigation shall be reviewed by the CIA Director of Personnel Security or successor office to ensure uniform application of DCID 1/14 security criteria. The granting access approvals shall be coordinated with the appropriate program managers, as agreed by the DCI.

8.3.2 Staff personnel in the legislative branch receiving SCI access approvals shall be provided appropriate security briefings by the CIA and shall sign NdAs before receiving SCI access. SCI access approvals shall be recorded in a community wide database. Copies of NdAs shall be provided to program managers who request them.

8.3.3 The DCI's OCA shall be notified promptly of employee job changes or terminations to ensure debriefing of employees who no longer require access and to ensure updating of a community wide data base. SCI access approvals for legislative branch employees must be withdrawn if an employee leaves the specific position for which access was authorized. If SCI access is required in the new position, a new need-to-know determination is required

8.3.4 SCI shall be made available to committee and subcommittee members only through or under the authority of the Chairman of the Congressional committee or subcommittee concerned.

8.4 Handling and Storage of SCI.

8.4.1 Any executive branch component that provides SCI to Congress shall ensure that the handling and storage of such information conforms to the requirements of DCID 1/21(see section 3.1) or successor policy statements. SCIFs shall be accredited by the CIA. Where adequate provisions cannot be made for the handling and storage of SCI, no such information may be provided without the approval of the DCI.

8.4.2 Testimony or briefings involving SCI provided to persons in the legislative branch shall be subject to the following security measures:

8.4.2.1 Thorough physical security and technical surveillance countermeasures will be conducted in accordance with DCID 1/21 and DCID 1/22.

8.4.2.2 All persons present, other than elected officials, including transcribers and other clerical personnel, must be certified for access to the SCI being discussed. Arrangements shall be made to monitor entrances to the room where the presentation will be given to exclude unauthorized persons.

8.4.2.3 All transcriptions or notes that result from briefings or testimony must be handled and stored according to the SCI security requirements as specified in section 8.4.1.

8.4.2.4 The room in which a presentation is given must be inspected after the presentation to ensure that all SCI is properly secured.

8.4.2.5 Any IC organization that provides SCI to a Congressional committee, other than a committee routinely involved in the oversight and appropriations processes of IC organizations, shall endeavor to provide such information through the SSCI or HPSCI, as appropriate. The SSCI and HPSCI both have facilities that meet the DCID 1/21 requirements and personnel trained in SCI handling procedures.

The committee requesting the information should contact the HPSCI or SSCI and obtain permission to use their facilities prior to the transmittal of the information. Where possible, the IC organization concerned should retain custody of the SCI. Where the information must be physically transferred, arrangements shall be made beforehand to eliminate or minimize the risk of exposure of SCI sources and methods. Records of the transfer shall be maintained by the department or agency providing the information.

8.5 **Marking SCI Released to Congress.** SCI being prepared for release to members of Congress and Congressional committees shall be marked with all applicable classifications, SCI caveats, codewords, project indicators, and DCID 1/7 control markings. The term "SENSITIVE" may not be used instead of, or in addition to, SCI markings, as it does not convey the nature or extent of the sensitivities involved. Releasing agencies shall ensure, through their legislative offices or comparable elements, that Congressional committee staff employees, through their legislative offices or comparable elements, that Congressional committee staff employees, and employees of the Library of Congress and the General Accounting Office, have clearances and SCI access authorizations appropriate for receipt of the material involved. Releasing agencies also shall ensure that SCI being provided legislative branch components is stored in accredited SCIFs.

9.0 JUDICIAL BRANCH ACCESS TO SCI

9.1 **Policy.** Pursuant to the Classified Information Procedures Act of 1980 (CIPA) (Public Law 96-456, 94 Stat. 2025 18 U.S.C. Appendix 4) and the "Security Procedures Established Pursuant to Public Law 96-456, 94 Stat. 2025 18 U.S.C. Appendix 4, By The Chief Justice of the United States For The Protection of Classified Information," dated 12 February 1981, arrangements for the care, custody, and control of SCI material involved in any Federal criminal case shall be the responsibility of the Department of Justice (DoJ) Security Officer in coordination with the appropriate executive branch agency security representative.

9.1.1 Federal District and Circuit Court Judges and Supreme Court Justices are the only judicial branch employees who are exempt from routine security clearance processing. All other judicial branch personnel must receive a security clearance as provided for in the Security Procedures issued pursuant to the Classified Information Procedures Act.

9.1.2 The government may obtain, consistent with the CIPA and its Security Procedures, as much information as possible in its attempt to make an adjudication pursuant to DCID 1/14 for individuals acting for the defense.

9.1.3 There is no requirement for investigation or SCI access authorization for members of the federal juries. At a minimum, the government will request the trial judge to give jurors a cautionary instruction on disclosure of classified information provided during the trial.

9.1.4 A Judicial Security Officer shall be appointed by the court from recommendations submitted by the DoJ Security Officer and with the concurrence of the head of any IC entity (or his/her designee) from which the case-related SCI originates. The Judicial Security Officer is responsible for ensuring compliance with the CIPA and all other applicable directives and regulations concerning the safeguarding of SCI, and for providing needed SCI security support to all persons involved in particular cases.

9.2 **SCI Access Requirements.** Requirements for SCI access approvals shall be provided to the security officer who shall notify the DoJ Security Officer. The DoJ Security Officer shall coordinate requirements with agencies/program managers involved.

9.3 **SCI Access Eligibility Determination Procedures.** SCI access will be authorized by the DoJ Security Officer, who is responsible for adjudicating the results of investigations required by DCID 1/14.

9.3.1 The court and other appropriate officials shall be notified in writing by the DoJ Security Officer of SCI access approvals.

9.3.2 SCI indoctrination briefings shall be provided by DoJ Special Security Center (SSC) personnel, or by an appropriately indoctrinated representative of the DoJ SSC.

9.4 **Handling and Storage of SCI.** Matters pertaining to the handling, storage, and disposition of SCI shall be coordinated with the security officer, who is responsible for ensuring that proper safeguarding procedures are established and that adequate storage is provided for the SCI pursuant to the CIPA Security Procedures and this manual. These matters shall be coordinated with the US Intelligence Community entities originating the SCI involved in the case.

9.5 **Additional Details.** Additional details/information may be found in the CIPA and/or the Security Procedures, which may be obtained from the DoJ SSC. Any question concerning interpretation of the CIPA security procedures shall be resolved by the court in consultation with the DoJ Security Officer and the appropriate executive branch agency security representative.

10.0 SCI SECURITY INFRACTIONS, VIOLATIONS, COMPROMISES, AND UNAUTHORIZED DISCLOSURES

10.1 **Reporting Responsibilities.** SOICs shall ensure that persons under their cognizance are initially instructed and periodically reminded to report to their respective SCI Security/Control Officer:

10.1.1 Any possible or actual security violation, infractions or compromise involving SCI. Individuals who learn of such circumstances, infractions or compromise shall take immediate action to protect SCI found in an unsecure environment until it can be restored to SCI control.

10.1.2 Publication in the media of actual or apparent SCI information. Respective SCI Security/Control Officers, shall report incidents through appropriate channels to the cognizant SOIC who will advise the DCI.

10.1.3 Any unauthorized revelation or exposure of SCI that might reasonably be expected to result in publication of the SCI.

10.2 Investigations. SOICs shall establish procedures within their organizations to ensure that all security violations, infractions, compromises, and unauthorized disclosures of SCI occurring in areas subject to their jurisdiction are properly investigated. Investigations shall be designed to determine if there is a reasonable likelihood that a compromise of SCI may have occurred, the identity of the person(s) responsible for the unauthorized disclosure, and the need for remedial measures to preclude a recurrence. The adjudication of security incidents will apply a risk-based analysis which will assess intent, location of incident, risk of compromise, sensitivity of information, and mitigating factors.

10.2.1 If a compromise is determined to have occurred, the cognizant SOIC shall immediately report it to the appropriate IC program manager. An investigation shall be conducted to identify full details of the violation/compromise, and to determine what specific information was involved, what damage resulted, and whether culpability was involved.

10.2.2 If the case involves an inadvertent disclosure, the SCI Security/Control Officer is expected to exercise his or her best judgment as to whether the interest of SCI security are served by seeking written agreements from un-indoctrinated persons to whom SCI has been inadvertently disclosed. If the judgment is that those interests are so served, the person(s) involved will sign an inadvertent disclosure agreement, and the responsible SCI Security/ Control Officer has reason to believe that the person(s) will maintain absolute secrecy concerning the SCI involved, the report of investigation may conclude that no compromise occurred.

10.2.3 The form of inadvertent disclosure agreement may be developed by SOICs, but shall, in all cases, be structured so that it conveys no classified information itself, emphasizes that there is no time limit on the need to safeguard the disclosed data, reminds the signer of the provisions of the Espionage Statutes, and commits the signer to certifying his/her understanding of the situation and to affirming that they will never, without proper authority, disclose or discuss the information with any other person.

10.2.4 Summaries of investigations and of related actions shall be provided to the DCI by the responsible SOIC:

10.2.4.1 When investigations show that SCI was inadvertently disclosed to foreign nationals or deliberately disclosed to unauthorized persons; or

10.2.4.2 When cases under investigation involve damage deemed significant by the cognizant SOIC - espionage, flagrant dereliction of security duties, or serious inadequacy of security policies or procedures.

10.3 Corrective Action. Investigating officers shall advise cognizant SOICs of weaknesses in security programs and recommend corrective action(s). SOICs are responsible for ensuring that corrective action is taken in all cases of actual security violations and compromises. Administrative actions imposed in cases of demonstrated culpability shall be recorded in security files of the responsible SOIC. Except in instances where immediate action is necessary, an individual found responsible for a security incident will be afforded the opportunity to argue in their defense prior to the implementation of administrative action. Remedial actions according to the severity of the incidents may be applied by the SOIC. These options may include, but are not limited to: oral counseling; written reprimand; suspension without pay for a period of one or more days, and a written reprimand; termination of employment. Security deficiencies determined to have contributed directly to the incident shall be corrected if possible. If not, full details and recommendations on corrective measures shall be provided to the DCI by the responsible SOIC.

11. PROGRAM SECURITY REVIEWS

11.1 Policy. Those SOICs responsible for accrediting the SCIF and/or for the information therein shall be responsible for aperiodic reviews based on risk management principle. Program security reviews shall be performed by persons knowledgeable of SCI storage, control procedures, and shall be designed to confirm that procedures and safeguards implement the applicable DCIDs. Contractors are encouraged to conduct self-reviews to identify the efficiency of their security program. Review results shall be retained in the files of both the accrediting and accredited organizations. In order to avoid duplication, every effort shall be made to accept security reviews by other joint users of the SCIF for validation of security compliance. These reports shall identify any deficiencies found and the status of actions taken to correct them. The security review reports shall be made available to the DCI or his/her designee upon request.